D0065088

HAIKU HARVEST

JAPANESE HAIKU
SERIES IV

TRANSLATION BY
PETER BEILENSON
AND HARRY BEHN

DECORATIONS BY
JEFF HILL

THE PETER
PAUPER PRESS
MOUNT VERNON · NEW YORK

COPYRIGHT
©
1962
BY THE
PETER
PAUPER
PRESS

FOREWORD

OF ALL the *haiku* I have read — in English, since I know hardly a word of Japanese — the three previous collections from Peter Beilenson's press, and his pen, in my opinion are the best, by far the best, translations. He brought each picture to instant life. He did not cloud nuance with words. And yet each poem is fully at home in our own language. Each has its own inner music, with the least alteration of content, no forced sentiment or emotion, no mere cleverness. Tenderness, irony, exuberance, vision, a listening, and always beauty — he sensed in each of these qualities a dialogue between this world and the world of the spirit, and he conveyed both image and echo.

Having so admired his three books of over six hundred *haiku*, when asked to complete his fourth, I was hesitant. I could only try to do what he would have done. Following his way of work, I read all the translations I could find, recited Henderson's phonetic Japanese versions for sound, absorbed Atasaro Miyamori's literal couplets and his sensitive notes, finally bursting out with what seemed the inevitable; what I felt the poet might have said in English.

In doing this job reverently in Peter's stead, I am grateful for the pleasant company of his friends, Basho, Buson, Issa, Shiki, and others of those old Haijin who spoke with such beautiful, evocative simplicity.

This should have been Peter Beilenson's book. He had just come to Basho's joyous shout about bringing a snowball in by the fire, when he died.

HARRY BEHN

HAIKU HARVEST

JAPANESE HAIKU
SERIES IV

SNOW WHISPERING DOWN
ALL DAY LONG,
EARTH HAS VANISHED
LEAVING ONLY SKY

JOSO

DUSK, ADRIFT AT SEA . . .
WHY LOOK BACK
AT THOSE LESSER
HILLS HIDING FUJI?

KIKAKU

OH THAT SUMMER MOON!
IT MADE ME GO
WANDERING
ROUND THE POND ALL NIGHT

BASHO

CHANTING AND HUMMING
GONGS IMMERSE
THE GREEN VALLEY
IN COOL WAVES OF AIR

KYORAI

SO COLD ARE THE WAVES
THE ROCKING GULL
CAN SCARCELY
FOLD ITSELF TO SLEEP

BASHO

WHEN THE AUTUMN WIND
SCATTERS PEONIES,
A FEW
PETALS FALL IN PAIRS

BUSON

MY DEAR PILGRIM HAT,
YOU MUST
ACCOMPANY ME
TO VIEW THE PLUM TREES!

BASHO

HOW HOT AND DUSTY
THESE SUNSTRUCK
COBWEBS GLISTEN
BETWEEN DRY BRANCHES!

ONITSURA

TWICE PERHAPS THREE TIMES
THE CHIMES OF THE RIVER
CHANGED . . .
OH WHAT A COLD NIGHT!

ROKWA

EYES, YOU HAVE SEEN ALL . . .
COME BACK NOW,
COME BACK TO THE WHITE
CHRYSANTHEMUM!

ISSHO

A CUCKOO CALLS
AND SUDDENLY. . .
THE BAMBOO GROVE
LIGHTED BY MOONBEAMS

BASHO

ON THIS WELL-WORN STONE
GARLANDED WITH
PINKS OF SPRING . . .
O TO DRINK AND DOZE!

BASHO

HE WHO CLIMBS THIS HILL
OF FLOWERS
FINDS HERE A SHRINE
TO THE KIND GODDESS

BASHO

MOONLIT FLOWER-FIELD . . .
DAYLIGHT GIVES IT
BACK AGAIN
TO A COTTON FARM

BASHO

IF I COULD BUNDLE
FUJI'S BREEZES
BACK TO TOWN . . .
WHAT A SOUVENIR!

BASHO

HAVING SPOKEN ILL
MY LIPS NOW
FEEL THE COLD OF
AUTUMN'S FATAL WIND

BASHO

SOME POOR VILLAGES
LACK FRESH FISH
OR FLOWERS . . .
ALL CAN SHARE THIS MOON

SAIKAKU

UNKNOWINGLY HE
GUIDED US
OVER PATHLESS HILLS
WITH WISPS OF HAY

BASHO

UNCHANGED BY AUTUMN'S
ICY WINDS . . .
THE CHESTNUT'S SHELL
STAYS GLEAMING GREEN

BASHO

MY EYES FOLLOWING
UNTIL THE BIRD
WAS LOST AT SEA
FOUND A SMALL ISLAND

BASHO

THAT WINTER WHEN MY
FAITHLESS LOVER
LEFT ME . . .
HOW COLD THE SNOW SEEMED

JAKUSHI

NO WONDER TODAY
ALL THE MEN NEED
MID-DAY NAPS . . .
O THAT AUTUMN MOON!

TEITOKU

CHERRY BLOSSOMS, YES
THEY'RE BEAUTIFUL . . .
BUT TONIGHT
DON'T MISS THE MOON!

SO-IN

AH THE FALLING SNOW . . .
IMAGINE DANCING
BUTTERFLIES FLITTING
THROUGH THE FLAKES!

OEHARU

THIS OLD HAT, STOLEN
FROM A SCARECROW . . .
HOW FIERCELY
THE COLD RAIN PELTS IT!

KYOSHI

THE OAK TREE STANDS
NOBLE ON THE HILL
EVEN IN
CHERRY BLOSSOM TIME

BASHO

POPPY PETALS FALL
SOFTLY QUIETLY
CALMLY
WHEN THEY ARE READY

ETSUJIN

WHEN A NIGHTINGALE
SANG OUT,
THE SPARROW FLEW OFF
TO A FURTHER TREE

JURIN

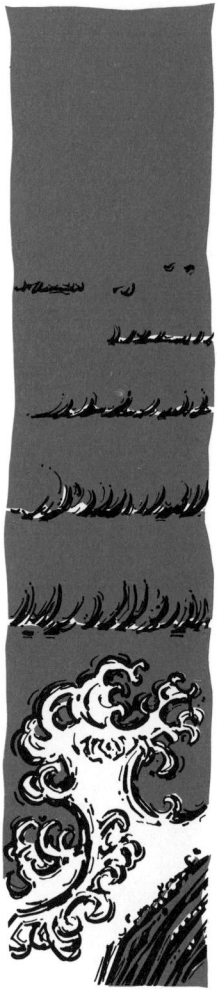

THE STILL SNOW WE
WATCHED . . . HAS IT
COVERED THE SAME HILL
AGAIN THIS WINTER?

BASHO

UNDER A SPRING MIST,
ICE AND WATER
FORGETTING
THEIR OLD DIFFERENCE . . .

TEITOKU

IF MY GRUMBLING WIFE
WERE STILL ALIVE
I JUST MIGHT
ENJOY TONIGHT'S MOON

ISSA

UNMOVED, THE MELONS
DON'T SEEM TO RECALL
ONE DROP
OF LAST NIGHT'S DOWNPOUR

SODO

WHO CARES TO NOTICE
CARROT FLOWERS,
WHEN PLUM TREES
EXPLODE INTO BLOOM!

SODO

DO THE TEA-PICKERS
ALSO HIDDEN
AMONG LEAVES
HEAR THE CUCKOO'S SONG?

BASHO

IN MY SMALL VILLAGE
EVEN THE FLIES
AREN'T AFRAID
TO BITE A BIG MAN

ISSA

OH THE FIRST SNOWFALL!
WHO COULD STAY INDOORS
ON SUCH
A GLORIOUS DAY!

KIKAKU

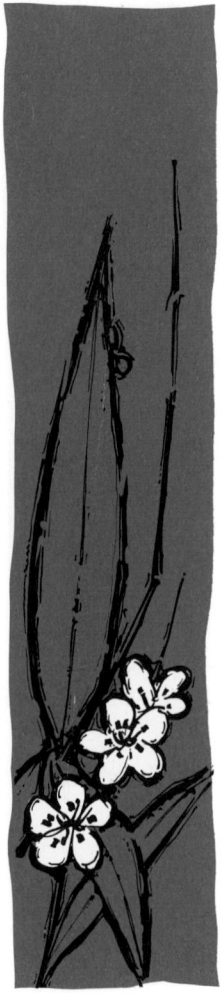

IN STONY MOONLIGHT
HILLS AND FIELDS
ON EVERY SIDE
WHITE AND BALD AS EGGS . . .

RANSETSU

WAKING BEFORE DAWN, SEE
HOW THE CONSTELLATIONS
ARE ALL
TURNED AROUND!

RANSETSU

AMONG THESE LOVELY
CHERRY BLOOMS,
A WOODPECKER
HUNTS FOR A DEAD TREE

JOSO

O THE TINY CRY
OF A PITIFUL
CRICKET
CAUGHT IN A HAWK'S BEAK!

RANSETSU

EVEN IN CASTLES
I HAVE FELT
THE SEARCHING BREATH
OF THE WINTRY WIND

KYOROKU

EVEN I WHO HAVE
NO LOVER . . .
I LOVE THIS TIME
OF NEW KIMONOS

ONITSURA

CUCKOO, DID YOU CRY
TO FRIGHTEN AWAY
MY MOTHER
WATCHING IN MY DREAM?

KIKAKU

NOW THE DRAGONFLIES
CEASE THEIR MAD
GYRATIONS . . .
A THIN CRESCENT MOON

KIKAKU

NEW YEAR DAWNING CLEAR . . .
CHEERFUL SPARROWS
CHATTER
ALL DAY LIKE PEOPLE

RANSETSU

PINE TREE SILHOUETTE
PAINTED BY THE
HARVEST MOON
ON A SHINING SKY

RANSETSU

WELL, THE FALL TYPHOON
HAS TAKEN
ITS FIRST VICTIM . . .
THE LOCAL SCARECROW

KYOROKU

A LEAF IS FALLING . . .
ALAS ALAS ANOTHER
AND ANOTHER
FALLS

RANSETSU

I'M VERY SORRY
TO HAVE TO DIE
AT THIS TIME
WITH PLUM TREES IN BLOOM

RAIZAN

HOW CAN A CREATURE
BE SO HATED
AS A WINTER FLY
YET LIVE SO LONG!

KIKAKU

POOR CRYING CRICKET
PERHAPS
YOUR LITTLE HUSBAND
WAS CAUGHT BY OUR CAT

KIKAKU

EVEN THE GENERAL
TOOK OFF HIS ARMOR
TO GAZE
AT OUR PEONIES

KIKAKU

EVERYTHING I TOUCH
WITH TENDERNESS,
ALAS
PRICKS LIKE A BRAMBLE

ISSA

A YEAR HAS GONE BY
AND STILL
I'VE NOT YET LEARNED
MY NEW MASTER'S NAME

RAIZAN

HELLO! LIGHT THE FIRE!
I'LL BRING INSIDE
A LOVELY
BRIGHT BALL OF SNOW!

BASHO

A TRILL DESCENDING . . .
BUT LOOK!
THE SKYLARK WHO SINGS
THAT SONG HAS VANISHED

AMPU

THINKING COMFORTABLE
THOUGHTS
WITH A FRIEND IN SILENCE
IN THE COOL EVENING . . .

HYAKUCHI

THE SUN HAS GONE DOWN
BEYOND A DEAD TREE
CLUTCHING
AN OLD EAGLE'S NEST

BONCHO

SNOW SETTLED TILL DAWN
THEN CEASED . . .
NOW SNOWFLAKES GLITTER
ON TWIGS IN THE GROVE

ROKWA

WITH A WHISPERING HISS
THE SCARECROW'S STRAW
SCATTERS
AMONG THE STUBBLE

BONCHO

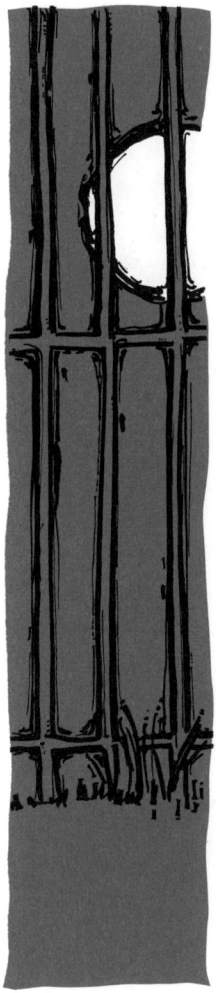

AN OLD SILENT POND . . .
INTO THE POND
A FROG JUMPS,
SPLASH! SILENCE AGAIN

BASHO

I MUST GO
BEGGING FOR WATER . . .
MORNING-GLORIES
HAVE CAPTURED MY WELL

CHIYO

WHERE DOES HE WANDER
I WONDER,
MY LITTLE ONE,
HUNTING DRAGONFLIES?

CHIYO

COOL GREEN GRASS . . .
ONE DREAM ALL HEROES
FIND TO BE TRUE
ON FORGOTTEN TOMBS

BASHO

WANDERING, DREAMING,
IN FEVER
DREAMING THAT DREAMS
FOREVER WANDER

BASHO

THE SEED OF ALL SONG
IS THE FARMER'S
BUSY HUM
AS HE PLANTS HIS RICE

BASHO

AUTUMN CRICKETS CRY,
KOSAI THE POET
IS DEAD,
HE NO LONGER SINGS

KIKAKU

ANOTHER NEW YEAR
AND MANY ANOTHER
FLEDGLING
WITHOUT A NEST...

ISSA

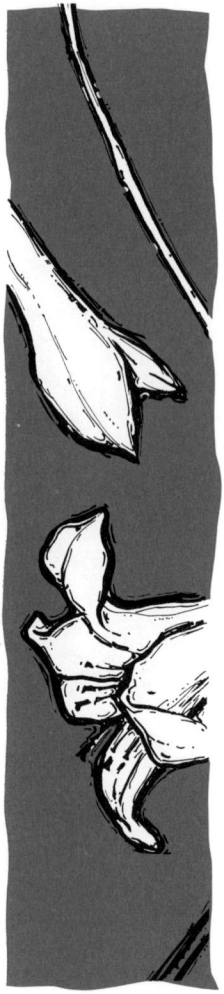

HOW COOL THE GREEN HAY
SMELLS, CARRIED IN
THROUGH THE FARM GATE
AT SUNSHINE!

BONCHO

FAREWELL! LIKE A BEE
RELUCTANT TO LEAVE
THE SWEET DEEPS
OF A PEONY...

BASHO

HOME AGAIN!
WHAT'S THIS?
MY HESITANT CHERRYTREE
DECIDING TO BLOOM?

ISSA

THE DRAKE AND HIS WIFE
PADDLING AMONG GREEN
TUFTS OF GRASS
ARE PLAYING HOUSE

ISSA

WHEN SPRING IS GONE, NONE
WILL SO GRUMPILY
GRUMBLE
AS THESE CHIRPING FROGS

YAYU

GAZING AT FALLING
PETALS,
A BABY ALMOST
LOOKS LIKE A BUDDHA

KUBUTSU

MY HORSE CLIP-CLOPPING
OVER A FIELD . . .
OH HO!
I'M PART OF THE PICTURE!

BASHO

HIGH ON A MOUNTAIN
WE HEARD A SKYLARK
SINGING FAINTLY
FAR BELOW . . .

BASHO

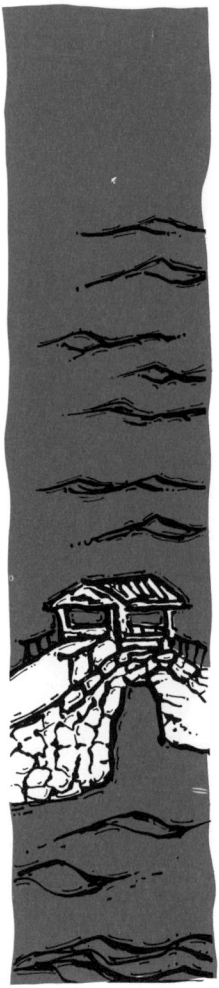

BEYOND PAPER WALLS
VOICES OF GEISHAS
WHISPER
ABOUT THE BRIGHT MOON

BASHO

THE STEAMING RIVER
HAS WASHED THE HOT
ROUND RED SUN
DOWN UNDER THE SEA

BASHO

SWALLOWS! THOSE HOMING
BEES IN THE SUNSET
BURDENED WITH HONEY,
SPARE THEM!

BASHO

OVER THE RUINS
OF A SHRINE,
A CHESTNUT TREE
STILL LIFTS ITS CANDLES

BASHO

IT IS NICE TO READ
NEWS THAT OUR
SPRING RAIN ALSO
VISITED YOUR TOWN

ONITSURA

AT LAST, WHEN HER SONG
IS STILL
THE GODDESS BECOMES
A SMALL GREEN BIRD

ONITSURA

A WIND-BELL TINKLING,
HUSHED IN THE NOON SUN
IS NOW
A SHELTER FOR BEES

GONSUI

WHAT USE NOW ARE TWIGS
BUT TO SWEEP UP
A LITTER
OF FALLEN PETALS?

BUSON

IN A WAYSIDE SHRINE,
A HUNGRY OWL
HOOTS AND HIDES,
SO BRIGHT IS THE MOON!

JOSO

ABOVE THE PILGRIMS
CHANTING
ON A MISTY ROAD
WILD GEESE ARE FLYING

RANSETSU

ALL NIGHT THE RAGGED
CLOUDS AND WIND
HAD ONLY ONE
COMPANION . . . THE MOON

BONCHO

HOW STILL IT IS!
CICADAS
BUZZING IN SUN
DRILLING INTO ROCK . . .

BASHO

WE ROWED INTO FOG,
AND OUT THROUGH FOG . . .
O HOW BLUE
HOW BRIGHT THE WIDE SEA!

SHIKI

FROM WATCHING THE MOON
I TURNED
AND MY FRIENDLY OLD
SHADOW LED ME HOME

SHIKI

WHEN MY CANARY
ESCAPED, WELL
THAT WAS THE END
OF SPRING IN MY HOUSE

SHIKI

A VOICELESS FLOWER
SPEAKS
TO THE OBEDIENT
IN-LISTENING EAR

ONITSURA

WITHOUT MY HAT! BAH!
WHY DOES THIS RAIN
HAVE TO PLOP ON MY PATE!
OH, WELL!

BASHO

BECAUSE SPRING HAS COME,
THIS SMALL GRAY
NAMELESS MOUNTAIN
IS HONORED BY MIST

BASHO

WAKE UP! WAKE UP! COME
SLEEPY BUTTERFLY
PLEASE JOIN ME
ON MY JOURNEY!

BASHO

LITTLE BIRD FLITTING,
TWITTERING, TRYING
TO FLY...
MY, AREN'T YOU BUSY!

BASHO

A SMALL HUNGRY CHILD
TOLD TO GRIND RICE,
INSTEAD
GAZES ON MOONLIGHT

BASHO

WHAT BLOOM ON WHAT TREE
YIELDS
THIS IMPERCEPTIBLE
ESSENCE OF INCENSE?

BASHO

PATIENCE, FROST!
AFTER THESE FEW
THERE WILL BE NO MORE
WHITE CHRYSANTHEMUMS

OEMARU

HOP OUT OF MY WAY
AND ALLOW ME PLEASE
TO PLANT BAMBOOS,
MR. TOAD!

CHORA

WASHING MY RICE HOE,
RIPPLES FLOW AWAY...
AS UP
FLY THE PIPING SNIPE!

BUSON

SPRING IS NEARLY GONE
SO NOW
THIS OLD CHERRY TREE
DECIDES TO BLOOM!

BUSON

FLOWERS IN SHADOW...
A MOON FLOATING
IN THE EAST,
IN THE WEST, THE SUN

BUSON

DAY DARKEN! FROGS SAY
BY DAY... BRING LIGHT!
LIGHT! THEY CRY
BY NIGHT. OLD GRUMBLERS!

BUSON

TIDES OF THE SPRING SEA,
TIDE AFTER INDOLENT TIDE
DRIFTING
ON AND ON . . .

BUSON

BEYOND THE TEMPLE
AND THE GARDEN LANTERNS,
SWANS
AFLOAT AND ASLEEP . . .

SHIKI

AS SHE WASHES RICE,
HER SMILING FACE
IS BRIEFLY
LIT BY FIREFLY

ANON.

A MOUNTAIN VILLAGE
LOST IN SNOW . . .
UNDER THE DRIFTS
A SOUND OF WATER

SHIKI

ONE MAN AND ONE FLY
BUZZING TOGETHER
IN ONE BIG BARE
SUNNY ROOM . . .

ISSA

WITHERED TUFTS OF GRASS . . .
ONCE UPON A TIME
THERE WAS, AND IS,
AN OLD WITCH!

ISSA

SINCE I FIRST BECAME
A HERMIT,
THE FROGS HAVE SUNG
ONLY OF OLD AGE

ISSA

THERE GOES A BEGGAR
NAKED
EXCEPT FOR HIS ROBES
OF HEAVEN AND EARTH!

KIKAKU

OLD MAN WITH ONE EAR
HELD CLOSE,
DO I SOUND TO YOU
LIKE A BUZZING GNAT?

ISSA

A SNOWY MOUNTAIN
ECHOES IN THE
JEWELED EYES
OF A DRAGONFLY

ISSA

HEAVY WAVES CRASHING . . .
SILENTLY
OVER SADO
FLOWS HEAVEN'S RIVER

BASHO

THIS IS MY OWN SNOW
THAT SAGS
MY OLD MATTED HAT,
AND IT'S LIGHT AS DOWN!

KIKAKU

HAWKS OVER THE SEA . . .
AS WE
IN OUR VILLAGE DANCE
IN SMALLER CIRCLES

TAIGI

WE COVER FRAGILE BONES
IN OUR FESTIVE BEST
TO VIEW
IMMORTAL FLOWERS

ONITSURA

THE LEAVES NEVER KNOW
WHICH LEAF
WILL BE FIRST TO FALL . . .
DOES THE WIND KNOW?

SOSEKI

MOON ADRIFT IN A CLOUD . . .
I HAVE A MIND
TO BORROW
A SMALL RIPE MELON

SHIKI

PREACH AWAY, CRICKET,
IT DOESN'T MATTER TO ME.
I KNOW
IT'S AUTUMN

SOSEKI

I MIGHT FEEL COOLER
IF I WERE THE
EMPEROR OF ROCKS
IN THE SEA

SOSEKI

SINCE NO BELLS RESOUND
IN THIS TOWN,
WHAT DO PEOPLE DO
ON SPRING EVENINGS?

BASHO

UNDER THE TEMPLE EAVES
GOLD FADES . . .
THROUGH BUDDING LEAVES
WE LOOK TOWARD THE PAST

CHORA

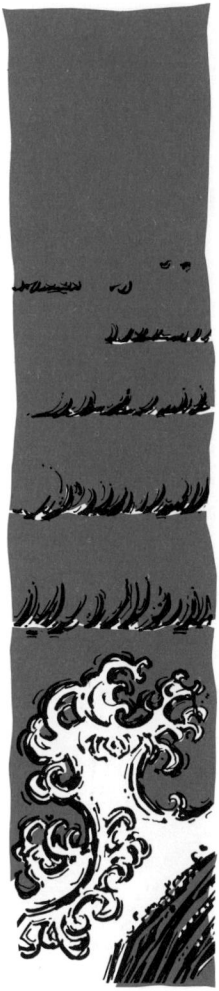

WHOSE DRESS COULD THIS BE
THIN ON THE LEAF-GOLD
AUTUMN SCREEN?
ONLY THE WIND'S

BUSON

ALL DAY IN GREY RAIN
HOLLYHOCKS
FOLLOW THE SUN'S
INVISIBLE ROAD

BASHO

JEWELS OF SMALL SHELLS
IN RIPPLES
OF SAND, TANGLED
WITH KELP AND RUBBISH

BASHO

AFTER BELLS HAD RUNG
AND WERE SILENT...
FLOWERS CHIMED
A PEAL OF FRAGRANCE

BASHO

BROWN LEAF FROM A TREE
UNKNOWN CLINGS
TO A STRANGE
GREEN-SPOTTED MUSHROOM

BASHO

LIGHTNING FLICKERING
WITHOUT SOUND . . .
HOW FAR AWAY
THE NIGHT-HERON CRIES!

BASHO

OUT OF ONE WINTRY
TWIG, ONE BUD,
ONE BLOSSOM'S WORTH
OF WARMTH AT LONG LAST!

RANSETSU

BEHIND ME THE MOON
BRUSHES
SHADOWS OF PINE TREES
LIGHTLY ON THE FLOOR

KIKAKU

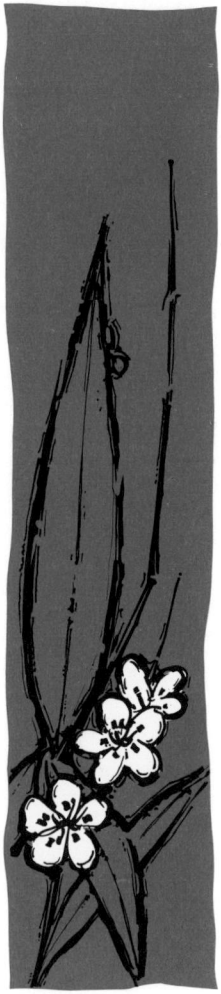

A NIGHT BRIGHT WITH STARS...
WHOSE GHOST IS THIS
WHISPERING:
SHALL I LIGHT THE LAMP?

ETSUJIN

RIPE HEADS OF BARLEY
BENT DOWN BY A RAIN,
BOWING
NARROW MY PATHWAY

JOSO

IT IS NOT EASY
TO BE SURE WHICH END
IS WHICH
OF A RESTING SNAIL

KYORAI

HO, FOR THE MAY RAINS!
FROGS SWIM
IN THROUGH MY OPEN
DOOR FOR A VISIT!

SANPU

AROUND THE GLOWING COALS
OF A BRAZIER,
OLD MEN TELL TALES
OF EARTHQUAKES

KYOROKU

OH HOW I ENJOY
EATING A RIPE PERSIMMON
WHILE DEEP
OLD BELLS BOOM!

SHIKI

FROG-SCHOOL COMPETING
WITH LARK-SCHOOL
SOFTLY AT DUSK
IN THE ART OF SONG . . .

SHIKI

ONE PERFECT MOON
AND THE UNCOUNTABLE
STARS
DROWNED IN A GREEN SKY

SHIKI

THE BEST I HAVE
TO OFFER YOU
IS THE SMALL SIZE
OF THE MOSQUITOES

BASHO

IF THINGS WERE BETTER
FOR ME, FLIES,
I'D INVITE YOU
TO SHARE MY SUPPER

ISSA

SLACK SAILS PUFFING FULL
GLINT ON THE SEA
IN A QUICK BRIGHT
WINTER SHOWER

KYORAI

UP FROM THE BOTTOM
OF AN OLD POND,
THAT DUCKLING
HAS SEEN SOMETHING STRANGE

JOSO

A THREE-DAY-OLD MOON
ALREADY WARPED
AND TWISTED
BY THE BITTER COLD!

ISSA

AT DAWN MY CASTLE
WAS STORMED
BY A FLIGHT OF DUCKS
QUACKING IN A MIST

KYOROKU

ONLY A CHIRPING
INSECT TOLD ME
IT WAS NIGHT,
SO BRIGHT WAS THE MOON

ETSUJIN

NOT UNTIL I'D LOOKED
A LONG TIME
AT THE NEW SNOW
DID I WASH MY FACE

ETSUJIN

SMALL BIRD FORGIVE ME,
I'LL HEAR THE END
OF YOUR SONG
IN SOME OTHER WORLD

ANON.

A RED LEAF FALLING,
SETTLING
INTO THE RIVER,
CLINGS TO A GREEN ROCK

JOSO

CALMLY FUJI STANDS
HIGH ABOVE
THE NEW LEAVES' WAVES
THAT BURY THE EARTH

BUSON

ON THE TEMPLE'S GREAT
BRONZE BELL,
A BUTTERFLY SLEEPS
IN THE NOON SUN

BUSON

WHAT A PRETTY KITE
THE BEGGAR'S CHILDREN
FLY HIGH
ABOVE THEIR HOVEL!

ISSA

A CROW CLINGS SILENT
TO A BARE BOUGH,
CAUTIOUSLY
WATCHING THE SUNSET

BASHO

HOW FAR THE SKYLARK SOARS
OVER
A CLOUD-MOUNTAIN
BREATHING-IN SUN-MIST!

SHIKI

IN THIS TOWN
WHERE I WAS BORN,
TONIGHT MY ONLY FRIENDS
ARE THE CRICKETS

ANON.

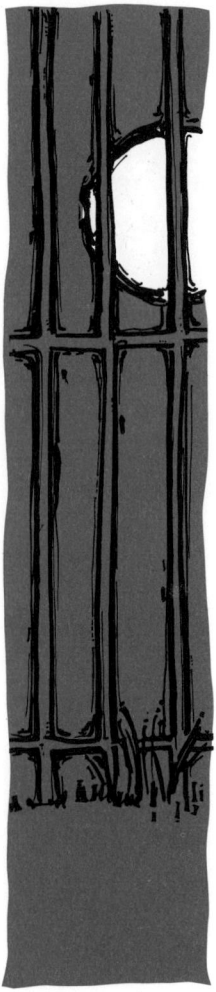

DEFTLY THE NEW MOON
BRUSHES
A SILVER HAIKU
ON THE TIPS OF WAVES

KYOSHI

RAIN FALLING AT DUSK
SWEPT ON, ON,
SPILLING MILLIONS
OF MOONS ON GRASS-BLADES

SHO-U

CHANTING A PRAYER,
MY HEART IS TWINED
IN GARLANDS
OF MORNING-GLORIES

KYOROKU

SINCE MY HOUSE
BURNED DOWN, I NOW OWN
A BETTER VIEW
OF THE RISING MOON

MASAHIDE

SCARECROWS ARE THE FIRST
HEROES TO FALL
IN THE RUSH
OF THE AUTUMN WIND

KYOROKU

BEANS FROM VINES
GROWING OVER A
SCARECROW
ARE EASY TO STEAL

YAYU

SHAKING HIS LOOSE SKIN,
A TIRED OLD HORSE
SCARES AWAY
A WHITE BUTTERFLY

ISSA

WHERE ARE MY NEIGHBORS?
WHY DO THEY SEEM
SO QUIET
THIS AUTUMN EVENING?

BASHO

UNDER A FULL MOON
ON A DISTANT
TIDELESS SHORE
I HEAR MEN SHOUTING

SHURIN

A POOL REFLECTING
WHITE CLOUDS . . .
DEEP IN A BAMBOO
SHADOW, A FISH STIRS

SHURIN

WHAT DOES THIS MEAN?
CHRYSANTHEMUMS
AND JONQUILS
BLOOMING TOGETHER!

SHURIN

BRIEFLY THE SUN SHINES
BRIGHTLY BETWEEN
CLOUD AND SEA
FADING AS RAIN FALLS

ONTEI

WHEN THE TIGHT STRING
SNAPPED, THE KITE FELL
FLUTTERING . . . THEN . . .
IT LOST ITS SPIRIT

KUBONTA

IDLY, A SHIP GLIDES,
THE TIP OF ITS SAIL
DIPPING
THE POLISHED WATER

OTSUJI

INTO A COLD NIGHT
I SPOKE ALOUD . . .
BUT THE VOICE WAS
NO VOICE I KNEW

OTSUJI

CAREFULLY PUTTING
HIS GOLDFISH BOWL
ON THE PATH
HE RAN TO A FIRE

GESSHU

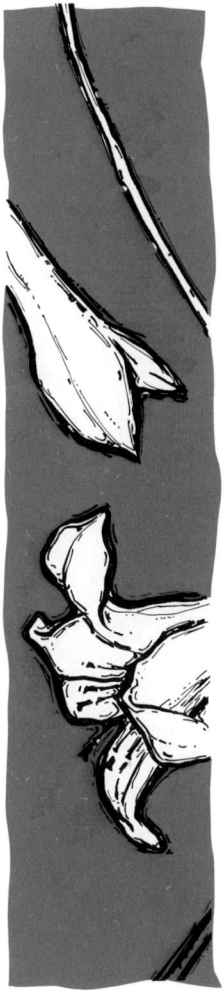

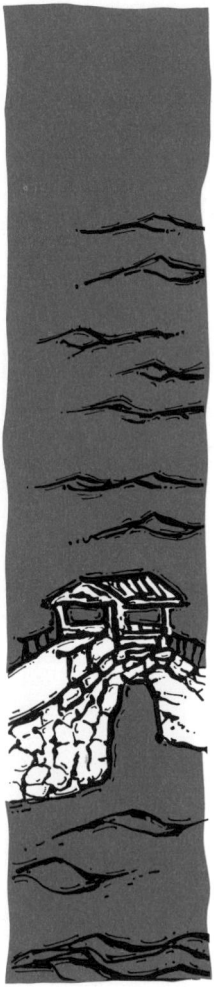

A HORSEFLY BUZZES
LOUD
IN THE SHINING HOLLOW
OF A TEMPLE BELL

BOKUSUI

OVER THE WINTRY FOREST,
WINDS HOWL
IN A RAGE
WITH NO LEAVES TO BLOW

SOSEKI

CUCKOO, IF YOU MUST,
CRY TO THE MOON,
NOT TO ME . . .
I'VE HEARD YOUR STORY

SOSEKI

BUTTERFLY! THESE WORDS
FROM MY BRUSH
ARE NOT FLOWERS . . .
ONLY THEIR SHADOWS

SOSEKI

THE MIGHTIEST GODS
LOOM NAKED
IN A BLACK WIND
LAUGHING AT DEMONS

SOSEKI

A RAIN CLOUD DARKENS
RED MAPLES
CLINGING TO CRAGS
BY A WATERFALL

SOSEKI

THE RIVER LEAPING
ROCKS, ANGRILY
ROARS AWAY...
AS THE MOUNTAIN SMILES

MEISETSU

BROKEN AND BROKEN
AGAIN ON THE SEA,
THE MOON
SO EASILY MENDS

CHOSU

EACH ELEGANT TREE
HAS ITS OWN NAME . . .
THIS BEAUTY,
THE NIGHTINGALE'S ROOST

SOSEKI

DREAMING OF SHOUTING
CICADAS,
I WAKEN PARCHED
FROM MY NOONDAY NAP

SOSEKI

HONKING WILD GEESE COME
SCRAWLING DELIGHT
IN SPRING'S COLD
PALE MORNING SUNLIGHT

SO-IN

BUTTERFLIES!
BEWARE OF THE SHARP
NEEDLES OF PINES
IN THIS GUSTY WIND!

SHUSEN

O MOON,
WHY MUST YOU INSPIRE
MY NEIGHBOR TO CHIRP
ALL NIGHT ON A FLUTE!

KOYO

I KNEW FROM THE SOUND
OF HIS TINKLING BELL
A PRIEST WAS THERE
IN THE MIST

MEISETSU

WATCHING THE SPRING MOON
RISE,
I NO LONGER BOTHER
ABOUT THE MOUNTAINS

KYORAI

UNDER A HELMET
HUNG IN A SHRINE,
A CRICKET
CHIRPS HIS LAST COMMAND

BASHO

I CALLED OUT: WHO'S THERE?
WHOEVER IT WAS
IN SNOW
STILL KNOCKS AT MY GATE

KYORAI

BEYOND THE MOUNTAIN
I WATCHED THE RAINBOW
PAINTING
THE SAGE'S VISION

MEISETSU

WHERE THE CUCKOO'S DARK
SONG CROSSES
THE SKYLARK'S CLEAR
HIGH SONG, THERE AM I!

KYORAI

THE SPEECH OF INSECTS
AND THE SPEECH OF MEN
ARE HEARD
WITH DIFFERENT EARS

SHIKI

A RED MOON GOES DOWN
LATE IN THE WEST . . .
SHADOWS FLOW EASTWARD
AND VANISH

BUSON

AFTER A SHOWER,
THE CLEARING SKY
SMELLS FAINTLY
OF HAWTHORNE BLOSSOMS

SHIKI

IN MY HOUSE THIS SPRING,
TRUE, THERE IS NOTHING,
THAT IS,
THERE IS EVERYTHING!

SODO

FOOLISH DUCKS,
YOU KNOW MY REEDY POND
IS OLD AND
WATCHED BY A WEASEL!

BUSON

WILD GEESE HAVE EATEN
ALL OF MY BARLEY . . .
ALAS,
THEY ARE FLYING ON!

YASUI

OVER THE DEEPEST
DARKEST RIVER,
THE FIREFLIES
ARE FLOWING SLOWLY

SHIYO

AS FROGLETS
THEY SANG LIKE BIRDS . . .
NOW SUMMER IS GONE
THEY BARK LIKE OLD DOGS

ONITSURA

THE SLIGHTEST BREEZE
BLOWS AND THE SKY'S DRY
SHELL IS FILLED
WITH THE VOICE OF PINES

ONITSURA

COME COME! I CALL.
BUT THE FIREFLIES
FLASH AWAY
INTO THE DARKNESS

ONITSURA

WARBLER IN MY PLUM TREE,
PERCHING THERE
IS AN OLD
CUSTOM OF YOUR CLAN

ONITSURA

EVEN STONES IN STREAMS
OF MOUNTAIN WATER
COMPOSE
SONGS TO WILD CHERRIES

ONITSURA

AT LAST! IN SUNSHINE
SPARROWS
ARE BATHING IN SAND,
FLUFFING THEIR FEATHERS

ONITSURA

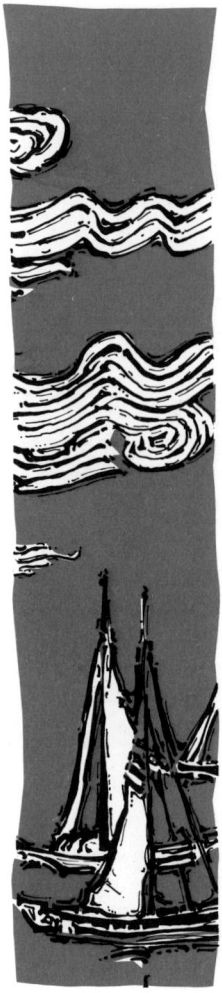

A TREE FROG SOFTLY
BEGINS TO TRILL
AS RAIN DROPS
SPATTER THE NEW LEAVES

ROGETSU

A DRIFT OF ASHES
FROM A BURNED FIELD,
A WAILING
WIND SIGHING AWAY...

ONITSURA

WHAT A SPLENDID DAY!
NO ONE IN ALL
THE VILLAGE
DOING ANYTHING!

SHIKI

WHY DO THEY WANDER
OVER THE GREEN HILLS
IN SPRING?
WHY DO THEY COME HOME?

SHIKI

BEYOND A DARK WOOD
LIGHTNING REVEALED
STILL WATER,
BRIGHT, LIKE A VISION

SHIKI

IF THE WHITE HERONS
HAD NO VOICE
THEY WOULD BE LOST
IN THE MORNING SNOW

CHIYO

LEAF FALLING ON LEAF,
ON PILED-UP LEAVES . . .
RAIN SPLASHING
IN POOLS OF RAIN . . .

GYODAI

ENVIABLE LEAVES,
BECOMING
SO BEAUTIFUL
JUST BEFORE FALLING . . .

SHIKI

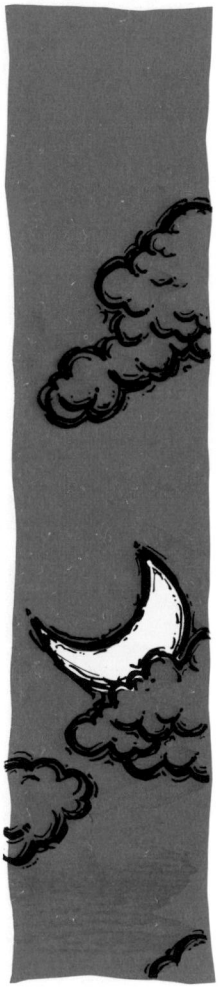

LIGHTNING FLASHING
ALL NIGHT IN THE EAST
THIS MORNING
SMOULDERS IN THE WEST

KIKAKU

THE ROOSTER, FIGHTING,
SPREADING
HIS RUFF OF FEATHERS,
THINKS HE'S A LION!

KIKAKU

A BABY WARBLER GAILY
SWINGING
UPSIDE-DOWN
SINGS HIS FIRST SONG!

KIKAKU

YOU FLEAS SEEM TO FIND
THE NIGHT AS LONG
AS I DO.
ARE YOU LONELY, TOO?

ISSA

THE SEA THIS AUTUMN
EVENING IS GREEN,
THE RICE FIELD
IS GREEN AS THE SKY

BASHO

WELL! HELLO DOWN THERE,
FRIEND SNAIL!
WHEN DID YOU ARRIVE
IN SUCH A HURRY?

ISSA

AS MOUNTAIN SHADOWS
DARKEN MY GATE,
THE TEMPLE DEER
STILL SEE SUN-RAYS

BUSON

HE IS UNKNOWN,
THE POET WHO SINGS
THIS GREATEST
OF ALL SONGS — SPRING!

SHIKI